INSTEAD OF GOD

INSTEAD OF GOD

A Non-believer's View of
Spiritual Realities

by

Andrew Solomon

Palamabron Press

Published in Great Britain by Palamabron Press
35 Hillway, Highgate, London N6 6AH

Copyright © Andrew Solomon 1993

British Library Cataloguing in Publication Data
Solomon, Andrew
Instead of God: A Non-believer's View of Spiritual Realities
I. Title
121

Printed in Great Britain by
Biddles Limited, Guildford and King's Lynn

ISBN   0 9522211 0 1

Cover illustration from Blake's 'Milton'

My thanks to Herbert Whone,
John Daniel, Adrian Theobald
and Douglas Falconer
for their helpful comments

CONTENTS

PREFACE

For most of us to-day the traditional religions of the West have largely lost their meaning. Though they evidently satisfied our fore-fathers' need to feel they could make sense of life, they no longer effectively serve that purpose for us. In their outward form at least, they are based on beliefs which stem from the distant past when it was easy to believe things which conflict with what we have since come to know. We have as much need as ever to find meaning in life, but it is useless for people who still manage to believe in those old teachings to urge the rest of us to go back to what, for us, is irretrievably dead. They might just as well urge us to return to the innocence of childhood. We need a different vision now, suitable for a different, less innocent, age.

A more modern orthodoxy, that of scientific objectivity, rejects the beliefs of the old orthodoxies as groundless; but it clings instead to a blind belief in reason as the only trustworthy mode of thought and dismisses all "subjective" experience as unscientific, best ignored if it cannot be explained away. So it turns its back on any feeling we might have that our lives are meaningful or enjoyable or that there is a spiritual side to them. Yet "subjective" feelings undoubtedly play as real and important a part in our lives as "objective" knowledge and need to be treated

1

just as seriously. Unfortunately we have at present no recognised orthodoxy which looks squarely and honestly at both of these aspects of reality.

There is an utterly indescribable source of meaning, central to our being and to all our motivation, which can be directly known, yet which is quite beyond the reach of reason. I would say that the proper function of religion is to harmonise this indefinable subjective perception with our rational understanding. The old way of doing this was to attach it to an object - an idol - or a visualised image, which comes to much the same thing. This gives it a false objectivity which may make its value easier to grasp, but misses the truth in both directions. Judaeo-Christian religion worships a mere reflection of it called "God", an image projected as if it were somewhere else, as if we could disengage ourselves from it; and this reflection is itself hopelessly falsified by rationalised belief.

Many individuals have their own personal solutions to the problem. Some have turned to eastern philosophies which offer a much more subtle and highly developed understanding of the subjective and the spiritual; but they do so in terms of a very different cultural background. There is much that we can learn from the East, but for this we need not turn ourselves, as some would, into imitation Indians, Chinese or Japanese by slavishly following their traditions. We start from a different place and we surely can and should build on our own modern western foundations, digesting and assimilating all

2

the wisdom that we can glean from those exotic sources, from ancient western esoteric traditions or indeed from anywhere else whatever, so that we come to understand it in our own terms.

In what follows there are ideas gathered from here, there and everywhere, notably from Jung, from Blake, from Buddhist and Hindu philosophies, from the Bible and the symbolism of biblical and classical myths and even of the operas of Wagner. All of these are sources of universal truths, and very often they express the same truths in different terms, so that I find it hard to say where any particular thought may have come from. Over the years these ideas have grown together into what I believe is a coherent overall view which now seems to be my own. But there is nothing fixed or complete about this, and I can never be satisfied for long with what I have managed to write down. However, I hope that, with all its inevitable shortcomings, this brief account may be of some use to others who are also trying to make sense of life.

1.

VALUES, FACTS AND FICTIONS

How can we find a sense of purpose? Why is there so much ill will, misery and destruction in the world? What basis is there for moral values - why should we restrain any of our impulses and desires? Does anything really matter? What is it all for? Such questions trouble many people to-day who are disillusioned with the answers given by traditional religion but cannot find anything to take their place. And yet life goes on, often with zest and enthusiasm, sometimes with frustration and despondency.

It is not that our lives are really so empty and meaningless, but that we tend to look for the wrong kind of meaning. We should like to have a straightforward rational way of making sense of life; but there is no such thing. How could there be? Even the will to live is not rational. And we long for an impossible world without suffering and conflict. So we fail to notice the real meaning, the mainspring of life and the source of our enjoyment of it, which is something much less easy to grasp, but infinitely more potent than anything that could be constructed by the rational mind, not rational but numinous.

The Numinous

In the Concise Oxford Dictionary the "numinous" is rather unsatisfactorily described as "the combined feeling of attraction and awe characteristic of man's sense of communion with God and religion". This purely subjective feeling may have been bound up by the priesthood, perhaps to satisfy the people's need for a simple, straightforward, belief, with the idea of a God in human form, having a real objective existence; but the experience of the numinous cannot be truly described in rational, objective, terms (I should make it clear that though the ultimate meaning of words like "subjective", "objective" and "reality" is very elusive, for convenience I shall use them here in the ordinary relative sense on the level of what we have to treat as real for the practical purposes of living).

The impossibility of communicating any such inward feeling or perception without falsifying it is the central theme of Arnold Schoenberg's opera 'Moses and Aaron'. In the story of the burning bush Moses' vision was apparently of the fire of the spirit, something utterly beyond rational explanation, simply I AM THAT I AM. This is a telling image, but only an image. The reality of the experience, for which it can be taken as a metaphor, does not depend on any rational belief, nor is it confined to what is usually thought of as the religious field. It is indeed something that each of us knows in various ways, though we may not recognise its true significance in our lives. So how can we bring it into our conscious thinking? Let us look for a few pointers.

Many of us may have no religious belief, but surely everyone has a sense of the sacred, of an immeasurable value, whether or not he can find anything in particular to attach it to. Anyone may occasionally have an intense experience which is hard to describe, perhaps something like an overwhelming sense of beauty and significance; or simply of love; and we all find this value, if in a more diluted form, through ordinary human relationships and everyday events. We may also know it as that elusive factor in music, art or literature which is the essence of true art. I often feel it strongly in a great gothic cathedral even though I no more believe in the factual existence of the God to whom it is dedicated than in the historical accuracy of Botticelli's 'Birth of Venus'. It speaks in a general way of a *value* to which I must be true as a matter of personal integrity, following the demand of my deepest conscience, however erroneous the Church's teachings may seem to me as to fact and as to morality.

This sense of an unbounded value is real for all of us, however we may try to explain it, and it also appears very often in negative form in feelings of hatred and disgust. Behind these too there lies the power of a meaningfulness beyond all reason. Whatever form it takes, this is something we all know in ourselves as a feeling, not a matter of belief; and knowing is infinitely stronger than believing. In varying degrees of intensity it is the essence of everything that we want - it is the essence of wanting, or will, itself - yet our rational minds have no direct way of grasping it. However real this feeling is, it is tantalisingly out of reach of reason; and this is the source of the perennial problem. Yet it is in this mysterious elusiveness that its power lies.

Reason and the Numinous

The problem is that to have any sense of purpose and commitment in our lives we need somehow to bring this indefinable feeling of value into the process by which we guide ourselves; and to the extent that we guide ourselves by reason we need some way of linking it to our rational understanding. This has been the function of religion. Men have invented idols and gods, images to which the numinous value can be attached so as to give it a semblance of rational objectivity while preserving its mystery. The God of the Jews and Christians is no exception.

The original teachings of the Bible were presumably intended to provide a place for the numinous which could be understood by ordinary people of their time in terms of what they believed was objectively real; but there is much insistence on belief, much emphasis on "thou shalt have no other gods but me". Free thinking is strongly discouraged. Whatever the need may have been in those far-off days among relatively ignorant and primitive people, this is not good enough to-day. This great truth, the central reality of all being, is surely worthy of an intellectually honest attempt to reach it. It is true it cannot be reached by reason, but the deliberate and cowardly suspension of intellectual honesty entailed in belief is utterly unworthy of it, unworthy of what

Man is, disgraceful in the fullest sense of the word. It also involves the confusion of two different kinds of knowledge, objective and subjective, and the corruption of both.

The essential falsity of belief is reflected in the variety of the images to which different peoples attach this same highest value. A vast amount of hatred and strife is generated by these disagreements over something of such fundamental importance to the deluded believers.

Unfortunately, while our knowledge has changed enormously, those traditional teachings, having once been made sacred, have been preserved largely unchanged through countless generations, long past the time at which they were really appropriate to their rather questionable purpose. As they formed the basis for morality and for order in society there were powerful pressures on people to conform in their beliefs, pressures which are only now losing their force in some of the more "advanced" societies. But the new freedom of thought is a mixed blessing unless or until it can lead to a new popular basis for understanding suitable for our time. Meanwhile, for the individual, it leaves the choice wide open of where, if anywhere, to place the numinous value, and this has unfortunate consequences. Social cohesion is suffering, while within certain groups all sorts of dubious ideals, political and otherwise, are given the moral force of a religion.

Some make a religion of science, blindly clinging to the belief that it is the only way to any kind of truth.

That may be so as regards objective facts, but the objective facts with which science is concerned are only one aspect of what is real to us: in practice our feelings, our subjective perception of values, must play just as real and important a part in our decisions. We do know ourselves directly as purposeful beings pursuing ends of our own, following our likes and dislikes, desires and fears, as well as our intuitive moral sense, our sense of integrity. These are the things we have to live by; and we should try seriously to understand them and to see where they come from rather than allow ourselves to be carried along blindly, as most of us are, torn by conflicting urges and unconsciously ruled by prejudices. But in our outward-looking western culture there has been no development of understanding in this inward field of subjective values to compare with that in the outward field of "factual" scientific knowledge. It is this unbalanced development which has led to our present loss of direction. We have outgrown our inherited system of beliefs and values but have yet to establish a new one.

I think we may be able to do this is a way which, unlike the old religions, does not entail blind belief so much as a provisional understanding, a pointer which may help each of us to find his own way. In this inward field, what can be communicated can never be the absolute truth, and there will always at any time be many individuals who can see beyond it. We should not shackle our minds with fixed beliefs, but should each always seek to develop a deeper understanding which is truly our own. But whatever guiding principles we may arrive at which will provide a suitable starting point for this in our own time, they cannot be expected to serve for ever.

Subjective Knowledge

The phenomenal growth of scientific knowledge has been achieved by strictly *excluding* from consideration all subjective values, to the extent that "subjective" has almost come to mean "unreliable". To restore the balance, we must be able sufficiently to trust our thinking in that neglected field; and this means bringing to it a degree of rigour. This is not made any easier by the fact that subjective experience is inescapably private and cannot be directly passed on to anyone else. In this field each can only know his own truth and must find it for himself. This "knowing" is of the kind with which we know people, places, colours, tastes, sounds, fears and desires. It is different from that with which we 'know" facts; and in most languages other than English a different word is used for it. We cannot reach it through logical argument; but it has the certainty of direct cognition - for us it simply *is*, and needs no proof. But that does not mean that the constructions that we may build on it are necessarily correct or that we cannot deceive ourselves about it.

However, in order to think effectively about these "subjective" matters or to discuss them meaningfully, we do need to be able to place them within a rational framework; and the ideas out of which this framework is constructed will seem convincing or otherwise to the extent that they fit into place with everything else that we know as part of a self-consistent interlocking pattern.

Subjective values can be communicated with the help of evocative images; and there is a language of symbolism which we can apply to those images to bring them and what they stand for within the grasp of reason so that we can think constructively - and that means objectively - about them. Jung in particular showed how in this way the imagery of myths, which are of a universal character, could throw light on the general structure and dynamics of the psyche, while that of dreams and other personal material could provide clues, in relation to this general structure, to the inner state of the individual.

The situations presented in myth, fiction or dream arouse our feelings without involving us in outward responsibilities; so through them we can examine our feelings, our fears and desires, with a degree of detachment and, relating them to the general structure, consider the part that they may play in our lives - and whether they are based on reality or on delusion. We might gain a new insight, for instance, into how we attribute authority inappropriately to some people, and that could eventually free us of our unconscious, and possibly resentful, dependence on them. If such an insight *works*, if it produces an irreversible change of this kind - I mean not just a change of opinion, but a liberating vision leading to a change, however slight, of personality - it shows itself to be valid. A false idea will have no such effect, nor will a purely intellectual understanding, though that may be a necessary step on the way. To effect change, an insight must be "felt".

This personal enlightenment is cumulative: it cannot be destroyed - only error can be destroyed - but neither can it be passed on directly to anyone else. And it should always be borne in mind that if we would arrive at any sort of truth it is important not to confuse the two kinds of knowledge, "objective" and "subjective", or the kind of confirmation which is appropriate to each; and we must give proper weight to both. Though subjective truth, truth concerning our will, may be embodied in metaphorical guise in the symbolic imagery of myth, fiction and religious dogma, we should never confuse metaphor with fact: just because a myth, biblical or otherwise, may ring true with regard to values, we need not take it as true history; nor should we confuse the actual nature of existing objects with the subjective values which they may evoke in our minds as symbolic images.

2.

THE SINGLE SOURCE OF BEING

The Teleological View of Life

I have suggested that something like a revolutionary change is needed in our western approach to knowledge. Although modern physics has advanced into regions far beyond the reach of our senses where things are not so clear-cut, the conventional view of the function of science is still that it relates "effects" to "causes" according to apparently immutable laws. To assume, as some do, that the only truth is that which can be reached in this way is to reduce life to a meaningless mechanical process and to see ourselves as helpless puppets. It is deliberately to ignore, even to dismiss as illusory, the very thing that distinguishes the living from the non-living, that is to say, the presence of an active, initiating, will.

When Copernicus considered what we now call the solar system from a point of view which placed the sun and not the earth at its centre, he not only saw its structure in much simpler terms than before but also opened the way for Newton to discover the physical laws which govern it. Similarly, if, taking our cue from some eastern philosophies, particularly from the Hindu concept of the *atman*, we look behind the invisible internal functioning of our bodies, behind the conflicting parts of our conscious will and behind all our varied responses to events, we may see our whole being as emanating from the "sun" of a single active spiritual source. It then becomes possible to explain our psychological structure in teleological (end-seeking) terms as a clear, coherent, and relatively simple, whole.

Apart from anything else, though from a "scientific" point of view it proves nothing, if the idea of personal responsibility and integrity is to have any meaning, and I could not bear to live without a deep conviction that it has, it must surely require that each life be directed ultimately from a single source. If there were more than one source, if *within ourselves* we were motivated by different independent spirits, good or evil, planetary or terrestrial, or whatever, how could we be responsible for our actions? Who could we consider ourselves to be? There would be no hope of our ever achieving an undivided will.

This is of course not to deny that we are often possessed by what *seem* like independent spirits which upset our good intentions; but if, as I shall argue, these "spirits" can be explained as alienated parts of our own will deludedly pursuing false promises of meaning in life, we may hope to be able eventually to redeem them and to re-integrate them into a unified whole. In the East this aim of integration is widely taken for granted and is the main purpose of the many forms of yoga. Of course there are also innumerable unseen *external* influences at work, but they are part of the environment that we have to cope with, distinct from that one source of our being to which we are uniquely responsible.

16

THE SINGLE SOURCE OF BEING

What, then, from a teleological point of view, may be regarded as the structural centre of our own being? Is it not the universal principle of life itself? As I have already suggested, we recognise this from the outside, not only in other people and in our own bodies, but also in plants and animals, through the presence of a kind of active will or spirit. It is not essentially self-conscious, like our conscious will, though that is one particular manifestation of it, but is that more fundamental and universal force which causes each individual living thing, waking or sleeping, to live according to its own inborn nature, and to preserve its integrity.

According to some schools of thought "spirit" and "life force", or "libido", are two opposed principles; but I see them as opposite views of the same spiritual energy, which, when it acts through consciousness, is in effect the pursuit of the numinous. But looked at from the outside, whether in other living things or in our own bodies, or our compulsive desires, when it is directed towards aims which may conflict with our conscious intentions, this spiritual energy appears as unruly "libido". Whatever one may call it, it is that which, through the medium of the genes, gathers together matter to form the body in the first place, controls its growth and keeps it in being for a time according to its individual character and pattern of development and decay, so that the body may be regarded as an individualised expression of the spirit in material terms, tangible and visible. When death leaves it without that shaping will, it rapidly disintegrates.

17

There seems to be little room for doubt that this same life principle is the source of what we know from the inside as consciousness. However, it cannot itself be identified with consciousness, since it controls all those inner functionings of which we are quite unaware, and continues to do so when we are asleep. But again at death, when life leaves the body, so, apparently, does consciousness.

Indeed whatever it may be that lives through us, it is certainly something with powers far beyond those of the conscious self. To me it is a truly marvellous and inexplicable thing that, like millions and millions of other creatures, I have a body and mind of a complexity far beyond my understanding, an inexhaustible well of joy and suffering, of pleasure and pain. Where does all this richness come from - a richness which still exists even if one unimaginatively fails to realise it, even if one is blind enough to take life for granted as a boring fact of no significance?

Is it not the power of the numinous, the essence of will at the very heart of our own being, that is the driving force of the life within us? Surely it is a mistake to see that power as something like "God" from which we can exist separately.

This force acts through us on various levels, on the unconscious, physiological level, on that of instinct and on that of conscious choice; and on each of these levels one part of our will is directed to our own survival, well-being and reproduction. Though we may take such aims for granted - and we share them with all living creatures - they are not self-explanatory. Why should we want to live or to reproduce? On the physiological level we are driven by pleasure or pain to comply with those needs of the body which require conscious action on our part. But we as human beings are not satisfied with just that. We need something more to give meaning to our lives, to bring us an experience of the numinous worthy of our capacities.

Meaning through Creativity

We may have the feeling that something we do is "worth while", that it brings a satisfaction, a sense of rightness, which is more than just pleasure; but this feeling, however powerful, cannot be pinned down or grasped by the reason, not can it be reached by any merely mechanical means. I would say that for us it is to be found only through activity which in the broadest sense could be called creative.

As human beings we have creative imagination through which we seem to receive ideas and impulses from an unknown source, apparently within us, but no more controlled by our conscious selves than is our digestion or the circulation of the blood. We also have the faculty of reason, which gives us the executive power to put those creative ideas into effect. Something new then comes into being - we have brought about change. I would suggest that for our proper fulfilment we need to follow this urge to create and to give ourselves to it unreservedly, and that for us the aims of survival and of reproduction are only means to that creative end through which we can find the full experience of the numinous.

There are many different ways in which we can be creative, venturing into the unknown, thinking new thoughts. It is not only in what is specially thought of as creative work, as in the arts and sciences, that we can find this enjoyment, but also in using our ingenuity and imagination to solve quite ordinary problems - like how best to arrange the furniture or to express an idea in words - and in the use of skill and judgment in the pursuit of excellence. Creativity also undoubtedly plays a most important part in personal relationships, in the playing of games, particularly in the making of jokes and the exchange of banter, and in fun generally - there is always something playful about it, however serious its purpose and however formidable the power which it unleashes. We can all be creative in our own ways, according to our talents; and I believe that other creatures also have their ways of finding this meaning on their own level through the exercise of their natural capacities.

In most things that we do, most problems that we solve, our conscious purpose is to achieve a rationally understood, but generally prosaic, result. The concrete result may last; but the real meaningfulness of the action which led to it, the joy of creation, which may seem to come as a sort of by-product, can never be held on to. Yet life without it is empty - meaninglessly mechanical; so we pursue it continually, impelled ever onwards - we can never be fulfilled once and for all through any one achievement; but for each of us there is potentially a *way* of fulfilment, which in Chinese tradition is called the Tao.

This *meaning* is in itself universal and infinite, but as it acts through the individual, whether worm or man, it is conditioned and limited according to his particular limitations and his particular circumstances, which also determine the ways in which he can find it and the intensity with which he experiences it; but it still retains the numinous character which inspires the will. Like love, with which it is closely associated, it exists *between* what we see as within and what we see as without, between self and not-self, and not in either separately. It is at once the goal which draws us and the will which drives us; and always its unqualified, indescribable, reality lies beyond the reach of ordinary rational thought. This also means that we are easily misled by false promises of it which divide the will and lead to inner conflict.

3.

THE DIVISION OF THE WILL

Paradise Lost

There are two opposite directions in which we may seek *meaning*, and this is the primary source of conflict in the will: on the one hand there is the true creative path which is a hard, demanding, way of courage and self-denial, the way of discipline usually associated with father, and, on the other, the temptingly soft, easy, way of pleasure and self-indulgence more often associated with mother. Each of these opposite paths seems to offer a "meaningful" reward, even ultimately a promise of paradise; but only one of them is true to its promise.

Correspondingly we have two images of paradise, one of them the forward-looking image of the Promised Land or the New Jerusalem, a state of redemption to be attained, like the Holy Grail, only after the most arduous search, and the other, the Garden of Eden, the nostalgic, backward-looking, image of a former ideal state of innocence, from which we are irrevocably exiled, though we still deludedly crave for it. These images of paradise are only images, but they do enshrine real subjective values. Their symbolism, like that of the expulsion of Adam and Eve from Eden, can be interpreted in terms of the individual life so as to explain that continual conflict in the will which afflicts us in our state of symbolic exile.

The root cause of this conflict and of our exile can be found in our human capacity for reasoned thinking. Reason is essentially divisive, and is often symbolised by a sharp-edged, cleaving, sword. Existence in space and time is one continuous whole; but in order to think, and to communicate through language, we mentally divide up this whole into things and events and name these with nouns; and we further differentiate between these parts of what exists or happens by describing them with adjectives in terms of pairs of opposite qualities or attributes, such as light and dark, fast and slow, or good and bad. From these also stem pairs of opposite abstract nouns like pleasure and pain, strength and weakness, order and chaos. All these mental concepts are useful for achieving our practical ends; but our thinking is so conditioned by them that we usually fail to recognise that they exist only in the mind and that the opposites are meaningful only in a comparative sense in relation to each other.

Confusion arises particularly when we try to give these opposites an absolute meaning, when we want to have, or to be, one of such a pair without the other. As a matter of course we seek pleasure or comfort and avoid pain, we seek power and avoid weakness, while to be acceptable to those on whom we feel dependent, first our parents, and then society, we try to be good and not bad according to their values. But we might as well look for an object with a front but no back, a top but no bottom and a right side but no left. We persistently pursue the impossible.

In order to understand how this leads to exile from the infantile paradise let us look at the pattern of our development as we grow up from earliest childhood.

We begin life in the womb, where all our needs are met and no demands whatever are made on us. It is a paradise of total security and perfect innocence. But after nine months we are expelled from it into a separate existence. Even then it may be supposed that to begin with we experience this existence as a single undifferentiated reality, with no concept of self as distinct from not-self (see, for instance, Erich Fromm, 'Fear of Freedom' Ch. 2). Though it could perhaps be argued that as soon as we are born we acquire the instinctual ability to recognise a few things, such as the source of food, to start with, our empirical awareness must to all intents and purposes embrace everything just as it is, a continuous whole, without any of those mental and linguistic divisions which we later impose upon it. How indeed could we have concepts of any kind when we have no experience to give them meaning, when everything in the world is new and strange to us?

This way of seeing gives us no means of grasping what we need to know in order to think effectively, or to will anything, let alone to deal with the practical problems of living. At first we are entirely dependent on our parents, "contained" within their care and protection, innocent in that we are incapable of the kind of consciously willed action which incurs responsibility (in Indian terms, *karma*). Though we may act on instinctive impulse, such action is surely not self-conscious or thought-out.

25

This initial state of undivided being is represented by the symbolic image of the Uroboros, a closed circle formed by a serpent swallowing its own tail, a symbol of the Whole, of self-contained completeness, and also of the encircling womb. But, perhaps quite soon, we begin to divide up this whole in our minds, imposing on it those artificial concepts and categories of separate things and events which we can think about and deal with; and this inevitably includes the idea of self. We are then no longer ourselves fully identified with the Whole. And we find that this self has needs which are not always automatically supplied by the Other. And since our parents, on whom we depend for everything, are only human, if we assert ourselves and make unwelcome demands there may be a danger of antagonising them.To the extent that that is so, our will itself is divided between the will to get what we want and the need to be loved.

This is the beginning of inner conflict, of the expulsion from Eden (though this represents a process that will be repeated many times on different levels). In symbolic terms, the closed circle of the Uroboros begins to be opened up so that the serpent of our energy is left partly unsatisfied. Its separated ends take on the opposite polarity of those two opposite sides of the will, the mouth, active and assertive, the will to get what one wants, and the tail, passive and clinging, the need to be loved.

As we grow up and gradually become less dependent, we go through many further steps of separation from mother; and each of these steps can be symbolised as another birth, another expulsion from a protective womb. At each step forward we gain a new degree of independence and freedom and a greater burden of responsibility and exposure to the harsh realities of life. As progressively less of our energy remains within the closed protective circle of the "womb", more of it is polarised and enters into our divided conscious will. Step by step we develop the separate individuality and authority that we need if we are to play an active part in the world, but we fall further and further from innocence.

Paradoxically, progress towards individuality leads always away from absorption in self and towards greater involvement with the Other, without which the need to create cannot be effectively satisfied. The goal of this progress, like its starting point, is represented symbolically by a circle of completeness, but one formed now by *two* serpents head to tail, signifying that *meaning* is found through the creative union of Self and Other, with reciprocal giving and receiving. This Other may be, on one level, an individual of the opposite sex, but it is also the outer world as a whole.

If, as we mature, we grow in wisdom so as increasingly to realise our potential, an ever larger part of our polarised energy will be engaged in this creative purpose; and ideally we may hope to arrive at a new state of wholeness, or non-separateness, in which it is completely absorbed in a reciprocal union of love. There we are fully reunited with that other half of our own being from which we were separated as we developed the idea of a separate self. It is the sacrifice of this illusory and divisive idea of self or "ego" which is the condition of the return to oneness; and, though it does not actually involve a change of direction, this may be seen as the task for the second half of life. But most of us never complete this task of integration. Indeed in the ordinary modern culture of the West it is not even recognised as a meaningful aim. But this is changing.

We can envisage at both ends of the journey a state of oneness represented by a circle of unity, a blissful state of pure, unconstrained, spontaneity with no sense of a separate self, in which we should be free of all inner conflict and guilt. So we are torn between these two images of bliss and completeness, one drawing us forward towards actively creative fulfilment and the other deceptively pulling us back towards the passivity of the womb, though we can never actually go backwards except in make-believe or fantasy. This is why the ring is such a potent, but ambivalent, symbol, as, for example in Wagner's 'Der Ring des Nibelungen' or Tolkien's 'The Lord of the Rings'.

Every move forward along the way to independence, involves, like physical birth, the loss of a sheltering "womb" of dependence; and though this loss is really irrevocable, we are tempted at each step to try to hold on to the comfort and security of our dependence, hoping to escape the demands and responsibilities of our new separateness and the conflicts which they bring.

Life is complex, and the choices facing us are rarely a matter of clear-cut distinction between black and white. It is often hard to know which is the true way forward and which the self-indulgent fantasy, which, for instance, is a brave assertion of independence and which a reckless yielding to temptation, which is necessary self-discipline and which repressive timidity. We may even on occasion need to use the force of the backward pull to break down a barrier to our forward progress.

As dependent children we need the guidance of our parents. So in many ways we subordinate our judgment to theirs, knowing that we must trust in their superior wisdom which is based on greater knowledge and experience of the world. We attach to them a god-like authority and at first unquestioningly accept their values. At the time this is a proper exercise of our own judgment. But as we grow up and become increasingly capable of judging for ourselves, we are subject to a tension between the drive towards independence and the temptation to cling to the security of parental guidance. This tension is often reflected in a rebellious resentment against those on whom we are still unconsciously dependent and to whom we still attribute authority in spite of ourselves. For some children it is easier than for others to break away from childish dependence - for some parents it is easier than for others to let go of their domination over their children. To do so they need to be sufficiently secure in themselves to be able to accept and value their children's standing as separate individuals, to love them unconditionally and to help them increasingly to make their own decisions.

It seems that virtually no-one enjoys such perfect support that they are able to progress without ever looking back. To feel secure in our dependence we need to believe that we are really acceptable; and this means that we must believe in an image of ourselves, an "ego", which pleases our parents, or later on, the social group in which we feel we belong. So we dissociate ourselves in our own minds from whatever does not fit in with this image, suppressing the unacceptable parts of our will even though they may represent our true needs. In practice the resulting fictitious self-image is shaped not only by our parents' conscious values, but also very much by the hidden fears and compulsions that affect their behaviour towards us, and which they in turn no doubt, derived from their parents.

Compulsions

But we cannot really choose what to be or what to need. If we try to do so we fall into the trap of thinking we can be one of a pair of opposites without the other, "good" and not "bad". Whatever we have to

30

deny in order to believe in our "good" self-image, it does not just cease to exist. If suppressed it has ways of asserting itself indirectly, making us act compulsively against our adopted rôle in an attempt to compensate for the needs which it does not allow us to satisfy. But this compulsive behaviour is never a direct expression of what is suppressed - that would defeat the whole purpose of suppressing it. It is always a substitute for it. But indulging the substitute, though it may be pleasurable, can never satisfy the original need; so instead of bringing release, as the advocates of "permissiveness" in the 1960's would have had us believe, it brings enslavement to an insatiable desire, or else to an implacable resentment; and with it inevitably comes pain in some form or other.

The less free and secure we felt in the love that we received as children, the more difficult it is to let go of our dependence; and the more we suppress in clinging to our acceptable self-image, the more of our energy is deflected into those compulsive substitutes, that is to say, the more "neurotic" we are likely to be.

In symbolic terms, the greater our frustration, the more acute the polarisation of the serpent within us. Its two poles are in essence the two basic needs of active self-assertion and passive love. They can each be seen as an attempt to find again the lost original oneness of the tail-eating serpent either through swallowing or through being swallowed, that is to say, through a fantasy either of possessive domination or of surrender. If either of these fantasies is lived out in a relationship, there is outwardly only one effective will, one effective source of judgment, so that no conflict can arise. But under the surface the opposite impulse still exists, the other pole of the serpent, and, being frustrated and alienated, it takes on a more extreme, negative, character; and each of these suppressed impulses has its own way of taking over the conscious will at times, unnoticed.

The active will to dominate, the mouth of the serpent, can appear simply as the naked lust for power; but usually it takes possession of us surreptitiously, usurping the power of judgment. Very often it is disguised and justified as moral condemnation or righteous anger, seizing with hidden pleasure on the opportunity offered by someone else's wrong-doing. While masquerading as power and authority it is actually borrowing the authority of a higher power to compensate for a lack of individual authority. It is also associated with the conventional masculine rôle and very often given expression as a proof of manliness to compensate for hidden doubts; but this should not be confused with true manly courage. It finds a covertly pleasurable outlet in all kinds of aggressiveness, in bullying and sadism, or in personal and collective hatred, in persecution, mob violence and war, where its indulgence may seem to be justified in fighting a threat to order or to common values.

The impulse to submit, the serpent's tail, reflects a longing to give oneself once more to a perfectly loving mother who will satisfy one's every wish, a longing for passive pleasure. But this nostalgic fantasy is of a paradise irretrievably lost. However alluring the image, its promise can never be realised except in makebelieve. In a man, the way in which this force generally exercises its compulsive power is more devious than that of its opposite. Since he will usually suppress the will to submit, unlike that to dominate, as incompatible with his accepted masculine rôle, it emerges only indirectly as a craving for self-gratification, especially in the form of active sexual desire, consciously compulsive, for a woman onto whom he projects it. For her, a submissive rôle is conventionally acceptable (or used to be!).

In general, the compulsive kind of sexual interest, or lust, is aroused by people, actions or things, fetishes and so forth, associated with wishes that we hide from ourselves, wishes that we disown (and therefore project) in order to be able to believe in our acceptable self-image. It is as if some part of us wants in some respect to be that person who can acknowledge such a wish, and the force of the suppressed wish is displaced into a compulsive desire for union with the person. This avoids damaging the self-image by making the hidden wish conscious. In this way we hope to satisfy the undifferentiated longing which is all that we know consciously of any of our disowned needs. But this mechanism deceptively substitutes sexual pleasure as the conscious goal, an end in itself. It no more satisfies the original need than swearing cures a bruised thumb. Meanwhile the desire continues to be fuelled by that unsatisfied need. Just as compulsive aggressiveness should not be mistaken for courage, so compulsive desire should not be mistaken for love.

What attributes we regard as masculine and what as feminine, and therefore what attracts us sexually as the complementary opposite of our own self-image, is to a considerable extent determined by the social conventions by which we are conditioned, even by ephemeral fashions. Indeed more generally the dividing line between what we identify with and what we disown and project onto others can be drawn in many different ways; and this may go far to explain the many variations and so-called sexual deviations which occur, such as sadism, masochism, narcissism and homosexuality, most, if not all, of which would seem to be acquired, not inborn, characteristics, resulting from the outward pressures and problems of relationship in early life which affect the general development of the personality; but this is not to say that inborn characteristics may not predispose people to respond in particular ways to those pressures. There is much controversy over this, especially from people with axes to grind.

For a boy, a crucial step in his development is that in which at puberty he breaks away from his childish dependence on mother to be initiated as a man into the more demanding world of men, whose collective support he can then enjoy. This often involves a rite in which he has to undergo some kind of ordeal to prove himself. It is the onset of sexual potency which makes this separation from mother necessary. Having established his independence of her, he can return to woman in due course, armed with his own masculine authority, to relate cleanly to her on a more mutually challenging basis.

But not every man, or every woman, ever manages to achieve this truly adult kind of relationship. Much depends on how effectively their parents helped and encouraged them to grow up into independence.

The Moral Safeguard

As long as we are subject to those compulsive urges we need a stable source of moral guidance to save us from the folly, or worse, into which they could lead us. But the only morality that we know is that which gave rise to those compensating compulsions in the first place; and it must continue to do so as long as we identify with its values. It is apparently a vicious circle; and this pattern of two opposite compulsions with a third force of moral control pervades our lives as long as we remain in the "fallen", divided, state; and though as we grow up we gradually put more trust in our own judgment and accept more responsibility, even as adults most of us are unable to let go altogether of our moral dependence on an external authority. Indeed most people go through life without ever having fully grown up.

However, apart from our need for guidance as individuals, we also need a stable and orderly society in which to live; and that does require each of us to observe an agreed code of social behaviour. Such a code need really only amount to a set of unspoken promises between people, and the morality involved in this is that of behaving fairly and honourably towards others. However, in the Mosaic Law of the Old Testament this necessary social code was elevated to the status of a divine commandment, which, in principle, was inherited by the Christian churches. On the popular, exoteric, level at least, they taught of an external God as a judging lawgiver, a deified father-figure, however loving and forgiving, whose authority was absolute and who would reward or punish us in the after-life according to how in this life we had observed his moral law. This was certainly an effective way of getting people to stick to the rules; but it kept them, as it still keeps some, in a rather childish state of moral dependence and inward division.

For values to carry conviction they do indeed need the backing of spiritual authority, and with the decline of belief, this backing for the old system of morality is losing its force, with the result that social order is visibly and rather alarmingly deteriorating.

Yet in practice the threat of divine retribution has not been the only source of pressure to conform to the moral code. Its values have long been the traditional values of "society", the basis of social acceptability; so it has had behind it the very real collective power of society and the threat of social rejection. This threat still exists, as does the need to behave honourably towards other people; but the rules and values on which both of these are based are now uncertain and continually shifting. There is no longer a homogeneous social order in which everyone has his unquestioned place, no longer one universally accepted code which is above the divisions of generation, of class, of politics, of race or even of sex.

But there is another conception of moral guidance which from ancient times has been a part of most eastern thinking. The Five Precepts of Buddhism, for example, seem no different at face value from their counterparts among the Ten Commandments; but actually they differ from them in that they are not divine commandments to be obeyed on pain of punishment but advice on how to live without unnecessary suffering. Wrong actions are bad *karma* and automatically bring us suffering. Thus in wronging others we hurt ourselves inwardly. This is inescapable. Being untrue to ourselves, betraying our inner truth - for example, our capacity for love and compassion, or our courage to be true to our vision of necessity - brings pain, however little we are aware of its cause. Coming from within ourselves, the pain of this inner wound is immediate and automatic. If we know this we shall need no other prompting to seek the right way and to look for the true cause of our unhappiness, however unwelcome its discovery may be. But beyond each particular "sin" against ourselves there lies the general division and falsification of the will which results from identifying with received values; so our ultimate aim must be to heal this division, to become "whole".

4.

INTEGRATION

Paradise Regained

Becoming whole is really a matter of growing up more completely, of overcoming our moral dependence so that we can be more truly ourselves as sovereign individuals answerable only to our own inner spiritual authority.

So far I have described the process of division, the polarisation of the will, the progressive fall from innocence which typically takes place during the first half of life as we develop our grasp of outward reality and our effectiveness in acting on it. This enables us to build up a separate and independent outward personality and to claim a position in the world.

But we may be as yet only outwardly independent. As dependent children we gave over our own authority to our parents, gradually reclaiming it as we grew up; but most of us, though we may take it so much for granted that we are unaware of it and would probably strenuously deny it, continue to feel morally dependent on some imagined external authority even long after we have grown up physically.

To complete the process of separation which began with physical birth, and to re-integrate our divided will, we need to stop projecting parental status outside ourselves and to repossess fully our own authority. For this we must turn our attention inwards.

We all mature naturally to some extent as we get older. Illusions are destroyed and wisdom is gained through experience of life - we are often forced to accept responsibility; but in most cases this natural progress is limited. Those whose sheltering illusions have been shattered by exposure to exceptional hardship and danger often seem to possess a special strength and maturity, but for the rest of us it is all too easy to cling to our comforting illusions and our state of unconscious dependence. Even when we think we have understood it all, invisible barriers hold us back, barriers formed by unseen fears, by defensiveness, self-condemnation and guilt. To break them down it is necessary to force ourselves to look into the most painful places, to face what we are most ashamed of, to let go of that idealised view of ourselves which we have regarded as the condition of our being acceptable, the basis of our security. We have, in short, to break out of the vicious circle in which we cling to that false self-identity in order to protect ourselves from the compensatory compulsions which that false identity itself provokes. This is the main barrier that holds us back.

The aim of liberation through integration, though not foreign to western thinking, is, as I have said, more universally recognised in the East as the proper aim for everyone. But the road which leads to it is long and hard - there is no easy or painless way, whatever the false gurus may claim as they extract money from the gullible. Not everybody would readily choose to follow it. Some are driven to it by sheer dissatisfaction with their lives, perhaps starting with some form of psychotherapy; others would attempt it if they knew how; but the majority in the West are hardly aware of it at all as a meaningful possibility, or if they are, the thought of it makes them uncomfortable. They don't want to know about it. Perhaps they are aware of something unsatisfactory, even a bit shabby, about their lives, but accept it as a part of the normal human condition best left alone.

They tend to regard all that introspection as morbid and unhealthy. This is a poor excuse for evading the truth. But it is not a matter of dwelling on our conscious failings - that will indeed get us nowhere. To make any useful progress we have to get at what we are hiding from ourselves. We are defensive and vulnerable because of our unacknowledged guilt. We defend ourselves against even knowing what we are so ashamed of, our cowardice and our dishonesty, what it is that we run away from instead of facing up to. We don't want to know about any of it - it is too uncomfortable; and since we can't forgive ourselves for what we have not acknowledged, our suffering continues. We probably blame it on others, or on bad luck; but if we know that there is something we can do about it and that it is up to us to deal with it, we can surely accept the challenge gladly and stop pitying ourselves. It becomes much easier to face these painful things if we know that facing them will bring release.

But however daunting this work may sound, even in the early stages progress in it is rewarding and "meaningful" in itself; and it is clear that its benefits far outweigh the sacrifices that it demands - the sacrifice of cherished illusions. The ultimate inner truth is universal, but each of us can only find it for himself. Reason cannot reach it - it will simply appear gradually in its own way as the illusions which obscure it are removed. To expose these illusions, however, an active effort is needed, using all our faculties, including reason, feeling and, above all, imagination. But this is a very personal business in which each of us must face himself. Since we are all different, we each have different problems and obstacles to overcome; but these can all be related to the general structure which I have described.

Methods and Systems

There are many ways to self-knowledge, many systems, religious, psychological, eastern and western, some of which may be better suited than others to our individual needs; but there is something to be learnt from almost any of them. I shall not attempt here to describe any particular method, but will try to outline briefly in general terms what is involved in the process of integration. Some people may need personal contact with a teacher. Unfortunately there are many false ones around, and all too many uncritical followers who are happy to be led. Others may prefer to find help in books. There is certainly much that a reasonably intelligent person can do for himself in this way if he has courage, imagination and an open, but not uncritical, mind.

INTEGRATION

We must not imagine that we can know at second-hand the substance of anyone else's subjective truth. Indeed we should be wary of accepting unquestioningly any system, or of identifying with any teaching, which we have not properly digested and made our own. It is always important to distinguish between what one is told, and may accept provisionally as something to be considered, and what one really knows for oneself and in oneself. However, a genuine teacher will not impose his teachings but will lead his follower to see for himself. Even so, looking at the same thing from more than one viewpoint will often bring a fuller understanding than would be gained from any one source alone.

While we must be discriminating in what we accept, we should at the same time be as open as possible to new thoughts and always ready to root out our prejudices; nor should we reject ideas out of hand just because they come from a source which we do not fully trust. Valuable insights may be gleaned in quite unlikely places, and even ideas which we eventually find to be wrong can often lead to a profitable line of thought, or at least to a clarification of our thinking.

To get at what we have been hiding from ourselves we must have some way of circumventing the internal censor. One such method which I have already mentioned, developed particularly by Jung, is through the interpretation of dreams, fantasies, free drawings, paintings, poems or anything else that comes to us from a level beyond conscious thought.

43

For me, the existence of an inner source which was quite different from my conscious self made itself startlingly apparent when I learnt a method of free painting which allowed me to transmit something from that source without conscious interference. The results were far more powerful and vivid than anything I could have conceived consciously, and revealed feelings of a kind of which I should not have believed myself capable.

This imagery which comes from within ourselves in these various ways can be related to that of myths, which clothe in their symbolism the universal processes of the inner life. In this way it can throw light on our own inner state. This is perhaps more of an intuitive art than a scientific method, but none the less effective for that once the technique has been learnt (unfortunately it has been saddled with the somewhat misleading name of "analysis"; but both Jung and Freud were medical men who needed to sound professionally scientific).

Many of the new insights which can change our outlook will simply come to us of their own accord in a flash of intuition, but there is much that we can do to prepare the ground for them. Though an intellectual understanding will not in itself bring about any real change, clear and rigorous thinking can lead us to ask ourselves questions and to face feelings which we should otherwise avoid. Without that intellectual discipline these things could remain unfaced indefinitely as obstacles to progress.

The Healing Force

As this work progresses one becomes aware of the activity of a natural healing force, the unseen will of the inner Self to return to wholeness. To one who is open to it, it repeatedly brings, as if from nowhere, the very thoughts and feelings that are the key to the next step forward. And, if he has learned the language of dreams, it may sometimes carry on through them an illuminating dialogue with the conscious self. It is a source of wisdom to which he can appeal when perplexed, by looking deeply inwards, as in meditation or prayer. There he can find guidance - provided that he is honestly prepared to face the truth, however painful, and if necessary to let go of cherished illusions, to question any of the assumptions by which he has been guided hitherto.

Faith in this inner guidance is then seen to be the only way forward - anything else would be a self-betrayal and a folly. And this faith, based on, and repeatedly confirmed by, experience, is an inward strength securely founded on knowing, on utter honesty, not on the precarious self-deceptions of belief.

The Inward Observer

Whatever means we use, at every stage we have to face painful truths. Long before we are able to change our outward behaviour, in our private thoughts we can examine these things with some detachment, opening ourselves to uncomfortable ideas and thinking about them without committing ourselves or giving away our guilty secrets to anyone else, questioning and reconsidering all those received values and duties which we have taken for granted. Privately we may come to see that when all pretences are stripped away there is an irreducible rock-bottom reality of being: *"I am what I am; and who shall say that I should be different, that I should not be true to the essence of my own being?"* This thought brings us to the true authority of the spiritual centre. But there may be still much to be done and many illusions to be sacrificed, before this inward awareness can operate freely in our outward lives, where we may still be confused and misled by projections and compulsive compensations in our dealings with other people. All the same, this inward vision can become a centre of developing independent understanding which can grow in protected privacy until eventually it is ready to take over the control of outward life in place of the defensive and dependent self-image with which we have up till then been identified. From that moment onwards we shall have repossessed our own sovereign authority and judgment.

Meanwhile, the first task of this inward observer is to understand the nature of our dependence.

The pattern of our general adaptation to life is, as I have suggested, usually set in childhood as we relate to our parents, so it is very much influenced by their particular patterns of adaptation and their modes of relating to us. The more clearly we can understand them, the better we can come to understand ourselves. We may see how we have adapted our ways to fit in with them and have adopted their values and feel that we have to be a particular kind of person.

INTEGRATION

As long as we are identified with those values we cannot see what they are, being, as it were, contained in them, taking them for granted. But it is this unseen background of received prejudices that actually gives rise to our more visible problems. So we should use every means to uncover and question those prejudices, to develop a point of view that is outside them and free of the authority which imposed them. We should not be afraid to think outrageous thoughts. If we recognise that every so-called virtue gives rise to a compensating vice, how can we pride ourselves on any virtue? To rid oneself of a vice it is a virtue that must be sacrificed. Then one can be true to oneself and free of the inner conflict associated with that vice.

The Liberating Sacrifice

This may also be seen as letting go of the guiding principles of the safe and familiar self-image, the raft to which one has been anxiously clinging, to plunge like Jonah into the ocean of chaotic energies. As long as one remains divided, this is as daunting a prospect as that image suggests. The ocean of the numinous seems to contain all those dangerous compulsive forces from which one has been guarding oneself by clinging to that idealised self-image; yet it is that clinging to a fixed identity with its sterile ideal which itself makes those forces so uncontrollable. A life is a dynamic process of continual change - we no more have a permanent identity than has a wave in the sea.

Letting go of that self-image does not really mean losing all control. One does not, for instance, have to be morally identified with the social conventions in order to recognise that they exist and that it is a matter of practical expediency to take them into account. One is simply free to choose, to judge with detachment. Once one has ceased to identify with an ideal, the compulsive compensations disappear and one can ride the chaos with responsible awareness without being engulfed. At the same time one will cease to project onto others all those things in oneself that one had formerly disowned, so that one will see people as they are. One will be "born" fully into separateness and freedom, able to recognise the separate human reality of all other people, the divine value which lives through them, whatever faults and failings one may find in their understanding and behaviour. It is not just our own illusory fixed identity that must be abandoned, but also that which we attach to other people to cover over with undisturbing ordinariness the inexpressible marvel which is the reality of their being. To recognise this can only be to love; but it may be a kind of love which is hard to face.

Whatever else it could be, this must be a love which fully accepts the reality of separateness and the inevitable conflict of needs - not a soft love, nor a love that demands perfection, but a perception of sacredness. This is surely the proper foundation for morality. It can have nothing to do with any divisive judgment of good and evil but must lead always towards the realisation of *meaning* in the creative encounter with the Other.

INTEGRATION

The centre of our being is symbolised in many cultures as a tree, the axis of the world, the Tree of Life. Rooted in the earth, its branches reach up to heaven, linking heaven and earth (in some cases, as in the Cabbalah and the Bhagavadgita, it is inverted, with the roots above and the branches below). It is the place where eternity and time meet, an interface between the world of time and space, in terms of which we act, and that timeless reality of meaning which we find through action, the universal which lies beyond all that is merely personal. We must recognise that the proper function of the conscious self is simply to relate our perceptions of outward fact "on earth" to our intimations of the way to the numinous "in heaven", that is to say, to our direct perception of values - to love, not to arrogate to itself any other authority or responsibility. Then we are free to trust in the ever-renewed creativeness of the moment to carry us forward in perpetual change. Nothing is fixed or permanent. As far as I know there is no final goal - there is always something beyond.